Sally's red bucket

Story by Beverley Randell

Illustrated by Meredith Thomas

Sally played in the sand.
She played with a red bucket.

"Hello, Sally!
Come and play with me.
We can play with my ball,"
said Chris.

Sally ran to play with Chris.

"I will stay here
and read my book," said Mom.

The waves came up the beach.

The waves came up to Sally's bucket,

and they took it away.

Sally ran back to Mom.
"Look!" she said. "Help!
Come back, little red bucket!"
she shouted.

Mom looked up.

Mom looked at the waves.
"I can see your red bucket,"
she said.   "Come on!"

Mom ran to get the bucket.
Sally went too.
They ran into the waves.

Mom got Sally's bucket.

"Mom!" shouted Sally.
"Mom! Look at your book!"

They ran back.

"Oh, **no**!" said Mom.